FOR MOST OF MY LIFE I HAD FELT DISTANT FROM MY GRANDFATHER, PERHAPS MISTAKING THE LANGUAGE BARRIER FOR COLDNESS.

BUT AS ...
AGING ...
CEPTIO ...

I REALIZED THAT HE WAS VERY MUCH LIKE THE THING HE'D SPENT HIS LIFE MAKING: A HARD, PROTECTIVE SHELL CONTAINING HAIKU-LIKE WISDOM.

KRK

"YOUR LOVE LIFE WILL BE HAPPY AND HARMONIOUS."

CLAP CLAP CLAP CLAP CLAP CLAP CLAP

WASN'T THAT FANTASTIC?

LOOK AT ME... I'M CRYING!

MIKO! THANKS SO MUCH. CAROL SAID SHE COULDN'T HAVE DONE IT WITHOUT YOUR HELP.

OH, SHE DESERVES ALL THE CREDIT.

NOW DON'T BE MODEST. WE'LL SEE YOU AT THE BAR IN, SAY... HALF AN HOUR?

I DON'T KNOW IF I'M GONNA MAKE IT. I SHOULD PROBABLY GET MY BOYFRIEND TO BED.

OH, COME ON! I THINK WE ALL DESERVE A DRINK OR THREE. *HA HA*

WELL... I'LL TRY.

ASIAN-
AMERICAN
DIGI-FEST

WELL, I KNOW THAT PROBABLY WASN'T YOUR CUP OF TEA, BUT THANKS FOR COMING.

DID YOU REALLY LIKE THAT?

I GUESS IT WAS KIND OF CORNY, BUT... YEAH.

I CAN'T BELIEVE THAT WAS SUPPOSED TO BE THE BEST OF THE FESTIVAL. TALK ABOUT A BIG FISH IN A SMALL POND...

WELL, WE HAD MORE SUBMISSIONS THAN EVER BEFORE THIS YEAR.

YEAH... OF DIGITAL VIDEOS MADE BY ASIAN-AMERICANS WHO HAPPEN TO LIVE AROUND HERE.

DIDN'T THEY ALSO HAVE TO BE LEFT-HANDED OR SOMETHING?

WE WORKED REALLY HARD TO PUT THIS FESTIVAL TOGETHER.

I KNOW!

I'M NOT CRITICIZING *YOU*. I'M CRITICIZING THE SHITTY MOVIE. AM I ALLOWED TO VOICE MY OPINION?

YOU DON'T HAVE TO. YOU MADE IT PERFECTLY CLEAR WITH ALL YOUR FIDGETING AND GROANING.

I'M SURE THAT LING COULD HEAR YOU SNICKER-ING THROUGHOUT HER FILM.

IT'S GOOD FOR HER! YOU CAN'T CONTROL AN AUDIENCE'S REACTION.

WELL, IT'S A LITTLE EMBARRASSING FOR ME. AND REALLY, WHO ARE *YOU* TO CRITICIZE?

HEY...I KNOW A LOT MORE ABOUT MOVIES THAN SHE DOES.

I'M IN THE INDUSTRY...

"THE INDUSTRY"? YOU MANAGE A THEATER!

THAT'S RIGHT...A *REAL* MOVIE THEATER. WHERE NONE OF THOSE MOVIES ARE GOOD ENOUGH TO PLAY AT.

LOOK, IF YOU DIDN'T LIKE THE MOVIE, THAT'S FINE. I DON'T UNDER-STAND WHY YOU HAVE TO GET SO ANGRY.

BECAUSE EVERYONE KNOWS IT'S GARBAGE, BUT THEY CLAP FOR IT ANYWAY BECAUSE IT WAS MADE BY SOME CHINESE GIRL FROM OAKLAND!

I MEAN, WHY DOES EVERYTHING HAVE TO BE SOME BIG "STATEMENT" ABOUT RACE? DON'T ANY OF THESE PEOPLE JUST WANT TO MAKE A MOVIE THAT'S *GOOD*?

GOD, YOU DRIVE ME CRAZY SOMETIMES. IT'S ALMOST LIKE YOU'RE ASHAMED TO BE ASIAN.

WHAT?

AFTER A MOVIE LIKE THAT, I'M ASHAMED TO BE *HUMAN!*

OKAY, LET'S JUST... DROP IT.

:SIGH:

I WAS IN SUCH A GOOD MOOD...

CREPE EXPECTATIONS

I JUST HATE THAT SHE HAS TO TAKE A CONVERSATION ABOUT SOME STUPID MOVIE AND TURN IT INTO A PERSONAL ATTACK ON ME...

"A PERSONAL ATTACK"? GOD...I'M SURE SHE WAS JUST RESPONDING TO YOUR **CHARMING** NEGATIVITY.

WHAT AM I SUPPOSED TO DO...PUT ON SOME CHARADE AND ACT LIKE MY JUDGMENT IS JUST AS CLOUDED AS HERS?

I MEAN, SHE DIDN'T GIVE A SHIT ABOUT ANY OF THIS COMMUNITY... POLITICAL...**WHATEVER** WHEN I MET HER.

YOU'RE SO ARTICULATE WHEN YOU GET INDIGNANT.

OKAY...

CLUB WITH FRIES FOR YOU...

AND YOU'VE GOT THE TOFU SCRAMBLE CREPE.

THANKS.

I LIKE YOUR HAIR. IT'S REALLY CUTE.

REALLY?

I JUST CUT IT MYSELF. I WAS THINKING I SHOULD GO GET IT FIXED.

DO YOU KNOW WHAT KIND OF—

NO WAY!

I SHOULD GET YOU TO CUT **MY** HAIR SOMETIME!

HEY, SORRY TO INTERRUPT BUT...

CAN I JUST ASK... DO YOU KNOW WHAT KIND OF OIL THEY COOK THE FRIES IN?

OIL?

UH, I THINK IT'S CANOLA.

OKAY, THANKS.

WELL, JUST LET ME KNOW IF YOU NEED ANYTHING.

I WILL.

DO YOU KNOW HER?

NOT YET...

ANYWAY...I'M JUST SAYING THAT IT'S MIKO WHO'S CHANGED, NOT ME.

SO SHE'S GOTTEN A LITTLE MORE POLITICALLY-MINDED. I DON'T GET WHY THAT'S SUCH AN AFFRONT TO YOU.

IT'S NOT. IT JUST GETS KIND OF TIRESOME.

I MEAN...MAYBE I'D CARE MORE IF I EVER FELT LIKE I'D BEEN THE VICTIM OF SOME KIND OF...DISCRIMINATION OR SOMETHING, BUT...

YEAH, WELL...YOU LIVE IN, LIKE, THE MOST LIBERAL, DIVERSE CITY IN THE WORLD! YOU'D CHANGE YOUR TUNE IF YOU SUDDENLY FOUND YOURSELF IN ALABAMA OR SOMETHING.

I GREW UP IN **OREGON**! I WAS PRACTICALLY THE ONLY NON-ARYAN IN MY ENTIRE SCHOOL!

AND YOU NEVER FELT MISTREATED OR...DISCRIMINATED AGAINST?

OF COURSE! BUT NOT BECAUSE I WAS ASIAN.

IT WAS BECAUSE I WAS A NERD WITH A BAD PERSONALITY AND NO SOCIAL SKILLS!

YOU MIGHT HAVE A POINT THERE.

REMEMBER THAT GUY FROM THE DORMS... ELVIN...SOMETHING?

ELVIN WANG.

YEAH!

OF COURSE... THE GUY WHO BLAMED ALL HIS PROBLEMS ON RACISM.

EXACTLY! YOU'RE LIKE THE TOTAL OPPOSITE OF HIM. YOU REFUSE TO SEE—

OKAY, OKAY... ENOUGH.

PLEASE.

SO HOW'S SCHOOL? ARE YOU...

THE SAME. I'M NEVER GONNA FINISH.

I TRY TO STUDY, BUT ALL I CAN THINK ABOUT ARE THE INCOMING FRESHWOMYN.

THE WHAT?

THE FIRST-YEAR STUDENTS. THAT'S WHAT THEY'RE CALLED.

ARE YOU SERIOUS?

THAT'S WHAT THEY'RE CALLED.

OKAY, OKAY...

≈SIGH≈ THEY'RE SO CUTE AND NAIVE. MY GOAL IS TO AT LEAST MAKE OUT WITH A HUNDRED GIRLS BY THE TIME I GET MY Ph.D.

JESUS! I TOLD YOU NOT TO GO TO MILLS FOR GRAD SCHOOL. YOU'RE TOO WEAK!

WELL, WE ALL HAVE OUR PRIORITIES...

USED

OPEN

PSSHHH

CAROL THINKS THAT OUR ATTENDANCE MIGHT HAVE ACTUALLY **TRIPLED** THIS YEAR.

WOW.

AND THAT'S IN SPITE OF THE FACT THAT THOSE ASSHOLES AT THE WEEKLY REFUSED TO GIVE US A WRITE-UP.

UH-HUH.

HOW'S ALICE? DID YOU GUYS HAVE LUNCH TODAY?

YEAH. YOU KNOW... SHE'S HER USUAL SELF...

...PURSUING THIS GIRL, SLEEPING WITH THAT GIRL...

I'M STILL WAITING FOR HER TO SHOW UP SOME DAY WITH HERPES ALL OVER HER MOUTH.

IT'LL BE LIKE WHEN MY HIGH SCHOOL GYM TEACHER CAME BACK FROM SPRING BREAK AND SHE HAD ALL THESE—

OKAY... ENOUGH.

MM... THIS LOOKS GREAT.

DID I GET ANY MAIL TODAY?

YOU GOT A PACKAGE. WHAT DID YOU ORDER NOW?

I DON'T KNOW... MORE DVDs. I CAN'T EVEN REMEMBER WHAT MOVIES THEY ARE.

LOOK AT THIS...

THEY CALL THIS AN "IMPROVED DIGITAL TRANSFER"? AND WHERE'S THE GOD-DAMN EXTRAS?

PIECE OF JUNK...

DO YOU WANT TO GO TO BED?

ENH... I'M NOT REALLY TIRED YET. I SLEPT IN TODAY.

WELL, WE DON'T HAVE TO GO TO SLEEP RIGHT AWAY.

MAYBE I'LL COME TO BED IN A LITTLE BIT. I STILL HAVE A COUPLE OTHER DISCS I WANT TO CHECK OUT.

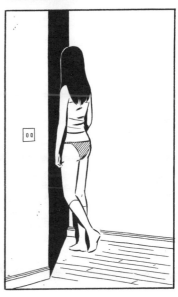

11

GENE, THIS IS AUTUMN. SHE'S JUST STARTING TODAY.

HI THERE.

OH, HEY. TOP FIVE FAVORITE MOVIES.

UH... WHAT?

I SAID, NAME YOUR TOP FIVE FAVORITE MOVIES. MINE ARE (IN DESCENDING ORDER): FIGHT CLUB, BOOGIE NIGHTS, JAY AND SILENT BOB STRIKE BACK, RESERVOIR DOGS, AND

GENE! LET'S TRY NOT TO SCARE HER OFF ON HER FIRST DAY, OKAY?

YIKES.

YEAH...SORRY. LET ME SHOW YOU HOW THE BOX OFFICE WORKS.

BEEP BEEP

HI! WHAT ARE YOU DOING HERE?

I WENT OUT TO DINNER, SO I ORDERED YOU SOME TAKE-OUT.

WITH WHO? YOU'RE ALL DRESSED UP.

JUST SOME OF THE GIRLS FROM WORK.

HERE...EAT BEFORE THE TEMPURA GETS SOGGY.

THANKS.

I'LL BE HOME AROUND ONE. YOU GONNA BE AWAKE?

I'LL TRY.

SORRY FOR THE INTERRUPTION.

SHE'S PRETTY.

YEAH. WANT SOME?

I'M FINE.

OKAY...I SHOULD TELL YOU THAT WE HAVE A LITTLE VIDEO CAMERA UP THERE, SO YOU'LL KIND OF BE... MONITORED.

I KNOW IT'S PARANOID, BUT...

ARE YOU GONNA BE WATCHING ME?

13

IT'S NOT THAT I DON'T TRUST YOU. IT'S JUST A THEATER RULE.

OH, I KNOW.

ACTUALLY, I LIKE BEING WATCHED. MY THERAPIST SAYS I'M AN EXHIBITIONIST BY NATURE.

OH... UH-HUH...?

YEAH...YOU SHOULD COME CHECK OUT ONE OF MY SHOWS SOMETIME. I'M PART OF THIS GROUP THAT DOES PERFORMANCE ART, SPOKEN WORD, THAT KIND OF STUFF.

REALLY? LIKE AT CLUBS, OR...?

YEAH... CLUBS, WAREHOUSE PARTIES...

BUT I DON'T KNOW... IT MIGHT BE TOO WEIRD FOR YOU.

WHAT DO YOU MEAN?

NO...THAT SOUNDS GREAT. YOU SHOULD DEFINITELY LET ME KNOW WHEN THAT'S HAPPENING BECAUSE... YEAH.

OH MY GOD... I AM *NOT* GOING TO HAVE THIS ARGUMENT!

IT'S NOT AN ARGUMENT. I'M JUST SAYING THAT I KNOW YOUR TYPE.

NO YOU DON'T, BECAUSE I DON'T *HAVE* A "TYPE."

O-KAY...

DO YOU REALLY THINK I'D BE ATTRACTED TO SOME GRUBBY, PUNK WEIRDO?

OH, DON'T OVERDO IT. SHE'S ALSO CUTE, WHITE, AND I KNOW HOW—

JESUS CHRIST!

YOU JUST *CAN'T* DROP IT, CAN YOU?

WHAT IS SHE... TWENTY? NINETEEN?

I HAVE NO IDEA! BUT IF IT'S SO FUCKING IMPORTANT TO YOU, I'LL BE SURE TO ASK HER!

WELL, I MUST'VE TOUCHED A NERVE.

YEAH...BY INSULTING ME AND, AND... INSTIGATING THIS STUPID *BULLSHIT!*

OKAY, WAIT...

GOD, I'M SICK OF THIS SHIT!

THIS ISN'T GOOD FOR EITHER OF US.

YEAH.

I THINK WE CAN BOTH MAKE AN EFFORT TO NOT LET THESE THINGS GET OUT OF CONTROL.

I KNOW.

LET'S TRY TO SAVE OUR ARGUING FOR SOMETHING REAL, OKAY?

THIS WAS JUST SO... NOTHING.

I DON'T KNOW WHY I KEEP PUSHING YOUR BUTTONS SOMETIMES.

I'M PROBABLY JUST TRYING TO GET SOME KIND OF REACTION OR SOMETHING.

WELL...I GUESS IT WORKED.

TCH...IT'S JUST EMBAR-RASSING.

I MEAN... THAT'S NOT WHO I AM.

I KNOW.

THANKS FOR DOING THIS.

IT'LL GO A LONG WAY TOWARDS KEEPING MY FAMILY IN DENIAL.

DIDN'T YOU ONCE TELL ME SOMETHING ABOUT YOUR PEOPLE HATING MY PEOPLE?

UH... HELLO?

DOES THE PHRASE "WORLD WAR II" RING A BELL WITH YOU? YOUR PEOPLE RAPED AND PILLAGED MY PEOPLE!

OH... THAT.

MY GRANDMA STILL REFUSES TO EVEN EAT AT A JAPANESE RESTAURANT.

STILL, I'M SURE MY FAMILY WOULD RATHER SEE ME WITH A JAPANESE BOY THAN A KOREAN GIRL.

I SEE...

SO RAPISTS AND PILLAGERS ARE PREFERABLE TO HOMOS.

EVERYTHING IS PREFERABLE TO HOMOS.

WHY DON'T WE JUST SAY I'M KOREAN WHILE WE'RE AT IT?

YOU KNOW... REALLY MAKE THEIR DAY.

ALL ASIANS MIGHT LOOK THE SAME TO *YOU*, BUT MY FAMILY WOULD SPOT YOUR JAPANESE ASS A MILE AWAY.

BESIDES... I DON'T WANT TO SATISFY THEM *TOO* MUCH.

17

HOLD MY HAND.

ARE YOU SERIOUS? JESUS, THIS IS—

SHH!

WHAT?

I TOLD YOU... GOOD CHRISTIAN BOYS DON'T TAKE THE LORD'S NAME IN VAIN.

I'M SUPPOSED TO BE CHRISTIAN, TOO? HOW FAR ARE WE TAKING THIS BULLSHIT?

SHH!

MAN...LOOK AT ALL THESE ASIANS!

:SIGH: HERE WE GO...

안녕 앨리스. 늦었네...

HI MOM...

HI DAD.

안녕.

이 사람이 그때 말한 그 남자친구야?

UH, YEAH...

MOM, DAD... THIS IS BEN.

HI THERE!

HELLO, BEN. I DIDN'T CATCH YOUR LAST NAME...?

UH... TANAKA.

VERY NICE TO MEET YOU, BEN.

IT'S GREAT TO MEET YOU BOTH!

그 남자가 일본인이란 말이야?

딱 보면 알지, 왜 몰라?

이런 뒷담은 안 하면 안 될 까?

왜, 그런거 물어보면 안 되는 거냐?

한국인이면 그냥 대놓고 얘기하지.

아이고...혹시나 했더니 역시나... 창피해 더이상 못 참겠다!

WERE YOU GUYS ARGUING, OR IS THAT JUST THE WAY YOUR LANGUAGE SOUNDS?

HEY...I SAID, WERE YOU GUYS ARGUING, OR—

SHUT UP.

ARE YOU OKAY?

I'M FINE.

THANKS FOR DOING THAT.

HOW WOULD YOU LIKE IT IF I WAS OBSESSED WITH PICTURES OF BIG, MUSCULAR AFRICAN-AMERICAN MEN?

YEAH, RIGHT... YOU REACH FOR YOUR PEPPER-SPRAY THE MINUTE YOU SEE A BLACK GUY WALKING TOWARDS YOU ON THE STREET!

I'M NOT JOKING AROUND, BEN.

LOOK...THIS STUFF IS JUST, YOU KNOW... FANTASY. IT'S **SUPPOSED** TO BE DIFFERENT FROM REALITY...OTHERWISE, WHAT'S THE POINT?

I MEAN, IF YOU WERE STRANDED ON A DESERT ISLAND, YOU WOULDN'T SIT AROUND DREAMING ABOUT SAND AND SUN, RIGHT?

YOU'RE NOT MAKING THIS ANY BETTER.

NO, LISTEN...

MY POINT IS THAT SAND AND SUN ARE **GREAT**, IT'S JUST—

DO YOU HAVE **ANY** IDEA WHY THIS MIGHT OFFEND ME?

IT'S LIKE YOU'RE OBSESSED WITH THE TYPICAL WESTERN MEDIA BEAUTY IDEAL, BUT YOU'RE SETTLING FOR ME.

JESUS...I'M NOT "SETTLING." WHERE DID YOU GET THIS IDEA THAT A GUY CAN ONLY BE ATTRACTED TO ONE "TYPE"?

WELL, I NOTICE WHAT YOU **GAWK** AT WHEN WE'RE OUT, AND IT'S ALWAYS SOME—

OH MY GOD...

21

OKAY! SO I'M BRAIN-WASHED BY SOME INSIDIOUS MEDIA CONSPIRACY INTO THINKING THAT BLONDE-HAIRED, BLUE-EYED WOMEN ARE ATTRACTIVE!

WHAT AM I SUPPOSED TO DO ABOUT IT?

YOU'RE A FUCKING ASSHOLE!

WHAT DID I DO? I *SAID* I'D THROW THE DVDs AWAY...

IT'S NOT LIKE I'M CHEATING ON YOU OR SOMETHING. I JUST—

ARE YOU SURE ABOUT THAT?

ARE YOU CRAZY? WHAT THE HELL IS WRONG WITH YOU?

STOP YELLING! WHAT ARE *YOU* GETTING SO ANGRY ABOUT?

BECAUSE YOU ALWAYS ASSUME THE WORST ABOUT ME! YOU NEVER GIVE ME THE BENEFIT OF THE DOUBT, AND YOU'RE ACTING CRAZY OVER NOTHING!

IT'S NOT "NOTHING," AND I'M NOT ACTING CRAZY, SO STOP USING THAT FUCKING WORD!

SLAM!

HEY, BEN...?

JESUS, GENE... HAVE YOU HEARD OF KNOCKING?

UH, LISTEN... AUTUMN WANTS TO RUN NEXT DOOR FOR A BURRITO, BUT IF I COVER FOR HER, THEN I'LL BE LEAVING HUMBERTO ALONE AT THE CANDY COUNTER, AND–

GENE!

I'M SURE HUMBERTO CAN HANDLE IT FOR A FEW MINUTES. TELL AUTUMN TO GO AHEAD.

HUH.

OKAY...

BOX OFFICE

23

...ANYWAY, THEY'RE TELLING US THAT WE HAVE TO LET THESE SEISMIC RETROFIT GUYS INSPECT THE THEATER, AND **WE** HAVE TO PAY FOR IT!

THAT'S ANNOYING.

DO YOU REMEMBER THAT INTERNSHIP I APPLIED FOR?

HMM...

THE ASIAN-AMERICAN INDEPENDENT FILM INSTITUTE?

I GUESS NOT. WHAT ABOUT IT?

WELL, I HEARD BACK FROM THEM FINALLY, AND... I GOT IT!

REALLY? THAT'S GREAT, I GUESS. WHAT DOES THAT MEAN? ARE YOU...?

WELL, THE THING IS... IT'S IN NEW YORK.

WHAT?

YOU DEFINITELY NEVER TOLD ME ABOUT **THIS**.

WELL, IT'S A FOUR MONTH PROGRAM.

FOUR MONTHS? ARE YOU KIDDING ME?

I KNOW...BUT IT'S AN AMAZING OPPORTUNITY.

WELL, FORGET IT.

WHAT ARE YOU TALKING ABOUT?

IT JUST SEEMS LIKE AN AMAZING OPPORTUNITY BECAUSE IT'S IN NEW YORK.

YEAH!

GOD...I HATE THE WAY EVERYONE IN THE BAY AREA WORSHIPS NEW YORK! TRUST ME: IT'S HIGHLY OVER-RATED.

WELL...

LOOK... THERE'S NO WAY I'M MOVING TO NEW YORK FOR FOUR MONTHS, OKAY?

I KNOW.

I WASN'T REALLY ASKING YOU TO.

WELL, MAYBE SHE WANTS YOU TO TALK HER INTO STAYING.

YEAH, RIGHT. SHE DEFINITELY DOESN'T WANT THAT.

SHE THINKS IT'LL BE GOOD FOR US TO HAVE SOME "TIME OFF."

SO ARE YOU GUYS, LIKE, BROKEN UP?

WHAT DID I JUST SAY? WE'RE TAKING SOME TIME OFF.

OKAY, JEEZ...

WILL YOU STILL BE ABLE TO AFFORD YOUR PLACE?

YEAH...SHE ALREADY GAVE ME HER HALF OF FOUR MONTHS' RENT.

OH, RIGHT... THE TRUST FUND. SO WHEN DOES SHE LEAVE?

END OF THE MONTH. TCH...NOW I'M SUPPOSED TO BE ALL "SUPPORTIVE" AND HELP HER GET READY.

GOD...

SHE'LL BE GONE BEFORE I KNOW IT.

WELL, THIS HAS BEEN FUN...

I'M GONNA GO PAY THE BILL.

Hegenberger Rd.
Oakland Airport

EXIT ONLY

THANKS FOR TAKING OFF WORK TONIGHT.

WHAT ELSE WAS I GONNA DO? MAKE YOU TAKE A SHUTTLE?

I THINK THINGS WILL BE PRETTY CRAZY WHEN I FIRST GET THERE, BUT I'LL GIVE YOU A CALL AFTER I GET SETTLED IN.

I'M REALLY GONNA MISS YOU.

TCH... IT'S ONLY A FEW MONTHS. YOU'RE GOING TO LOVE BEING A BACHELOR AGAIN.

YEAH, RIGHT.

COME ON... LET'S NOT GET ALL—

OH FUCK!

WHAT IS THIS? TRAFFIC AT EIGHT PM?

GOD *DAMN* IT!

HONK HONK

HEY, IT'S BEN.

YEAH, I JUST GOT BACK.

SO WHAT'S THE DEAL? ARE YOU STANDING ON A CHAIR WITH A NOOSE AROUND YOUR NECK?

NOT YET. I GUESS IT HASN'T REALLY HIT ME THAT SHE'S GONE.

OF **COURSE** I'M GONNA MISS HER. THAT'S NOT EVEN A...

YEAH...THE QUESTION IS WHETHER OR NOT SHE'LL MISS **ME**.

WELL, IF YOU WANT HER TO, THEN YOU'RE GONNA HAVE TO BE STRATEGIC. YOU CAN'T ACT ALL PATHETIC AND LONELY AND DESPERATE.

BUT THAT'S MY SPECIALTY! THAT'S WHAT I...

I KNOW. SHE MADE A POINT OF SAYING, BASICALLY, "DON'T CALL ME, I'LL CALL YOU."

NO, I THINK SHE JUST MEANT FOR THE FIRST FEW DAYS.

I KNOW.

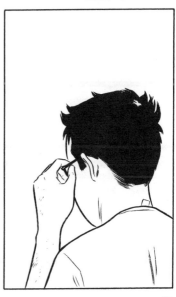

31

SKREEEE

32

TO BE CONTINUED